DEATH IS AS BEAUTIFUL AS LIFE; WE SIMPLY DON'T REALIZE IT UNTIL WE'RE HOME

BY:

CARLA DAVIS BONDS

DEDICATION

To my husband Vogel, daughter Shelby, my bonus son Andre and bonus daughter Diane.

ABOUT THE BOOK

This is a conversation from me to you about my unique upbringing and experiences inside a planet, a utopia, if you will, named Laclede Town.

First, I needed to research my ancestors prior to telling my story, for it is their blood which runs through my veins. Without my ancestors, I would not be able to introduce you to me and my story of life.

My ancestors had to endure great pain and suffering within an era of segregation, racism and out right inhumane treatment, simply because of their skin color.

My story will present an upbringing that is without delay, very much needed in each and every community around this country, the United States of America. The comradery experienced in our planet/utopia/community did not include racism, one's financial status, employment standing{s} or any other category that was the culprit of keeping a hatred of differences at the forefront of societies elsewhere.

Come along with me and experience the innocence, love, laughter, sadness, togetherness and common-sense upbringing I experienced within Laclede Town. I will always be forever grateful to the elders within our village. Under their watchful eyes we were taught how to respect them, one another, honesty, loyalty and most importantly, to love one another.

Ethel Blanks, my great grandmother was born on March 10, 1893 in Independent City, Missouri. She was affectionally known to us as "Mom-Mo". Ethel's citizenship status wasn't recorded. While African Americans were granted citizenship in 1869, their legal and civil rights were severely restricted for decades after.

1950 United States Federal Census

Name	Ethel Blanks abt 1893	Death: 24 Dec 1977 (aged 84)
Birth	Independence, Missouri	Burial Mount Olive Catholic Cemetery
Residence	1940, St Louis City, Missouri, USA	Lemay, St. Louis County Missouri USA
Residence	1935 St Louis, St Louis City, MO	Memorial ID: 47772772
Parents:	Unknown father/unknown mother	

She came to Saint Louis at a very young age. She found work as a Laundress, located in China Town. China Town was located on the outskirts of Mill Creek Valley. The majority of people living there were of Asian descent. Mom-Mo worked for several Chinese establishments. During Mom-Mo's employment, she began relationships with Chinese men. She married Floyd Anderson. Floyd's birth name was Ah Sing. He was born on July 15, 1887. His father's birth name was also Ah Sing. They both changed their names to Floyd Anderson. Both of their birthplaces were Hong Kong, China. They immigrated to Little Rock, Arkansas. Ethel and Floyd were able to get married. Ethel had four children, Elmer, Irma, Juanita (my grandmother) and Floyd Jr.

They lived with Floyd's family, his grandfather Howard Anderson, JD Anderson, Julietta Anderson, Fooyon Sing, Viola Sing, and Acuilla Sing.

MISSOURI STATE BOARD OF HEALTH
BUREAU OF VITAL STATISTICS
CERTIFICATE OF DEATH

37089

1. PLACE OF DEATH

County................................ Registration District No. _701_ File No. _10203_

Township................................ Primary Registration District No. _1008_ Registered No. _10203_

City................................ (No.)................................ St. _1_ Ward.

2. FULL NAME _Floyd Anderson_

(a) Residence. No. _706 So. 18th_ St. _7_ Ward.
(Usual place of abode)

(If nonresident give city or town and State)

Length of residence in city or town where death occurred _25_ yrs. ___ mos. ___ ds. How long in U.S., if of foreign birth? ___ yrs. ___ mos. ___ ds.

PERSONAL AND STATISTICAL PARTICULARS	MEDICAL CERTIFICATE OF DEATH

3. SEX _Male_ **4. COLOR OR RACE** _Colored_ **5. SINGLE, MARRIED, WIDOWED OR DIVORCED** (write the word) _Married_

16. DATE OF DEATH (MONTH, DAY AND YEAR) _October 23rd 1918_

5A. IF MARRIED, WIDOWED, OR DIVORCED HUSBAND OF (OR) WIFE OF _Ethel Anderson_

17. I HEREBY CERTIFY, That I attended deceased from _October 19th_, 1918, to _October 23rd_, 1918, that I last saw h. alive on _October 22nd_, 1918, and that death occurred, on the date stated above, at _6:15_ m.

6. DATE OF BIRTH (MONTH, DAY AND YEAR) _July 15 1887_

7. AGE YEARS _31_ MONTHS _3_ DAYS _7_ IF LESS than 1 day, ... hrs. or ... min.

THE CAUSE OF DEATH* WAS AS FOLLOWS:

11b Influenza (duration) ___ yrs. ___ mos. _4_ ds.

8. OCCUPATION OF DECEASED
(a) Trade, profession, or particular kind of work _Laborer_
(b) General nature of industry, business, or establishment in which employed (or employer)
(c) Name of employer

CONTRIBUTORY (SECONDARY) (duration) ___ yrs. ___ mos. ___ ds.

18. WHERE WAS DISEASE CONTRACTED

IF NOT AT PLACE OF DEATH

9. BIRTHPLACE (CITY OR TOWN) _Little Rock_ (STATE OR COUNTRY) _Arkansas_

DID AN OPERATION PRECEDE DEATH? ___ DATE OF ___

10. NAME OF FATHER _Ah Sing Anderson_

WAS THERE AN AUTOPSY? ___

11. BIRTHPLACE OF FATHER (CITY OR TOWN) _Hong Kong_ (STATE OR COUNTRY) _China_

WHAT TEST CONFIRMED DIAGNOSIS? ___

12. MAIDEN NAME OF MOTHER _Pettie White_

(Signed) _E. Allnworth_, M.D

13. BIRTHPLACE OF MOTHER (CITY OR TOWN) (STATE OR COUNTRY) _Unknown_

___ 19 (Address) _4059a Olive Str_

*State the Disease Causing Death, or in deaths from Violent Causes, state (1) Means and Nature of Injury, and (2) whether Accidental, Suicidal, or Homicidal. (See reverse side for additional space.)

14. INFORMANT _Howard Anderson_ (Address) _3005 Rawton Ave_

19. PLACE OF BURIAL, CREMATION, OR REMOVAL _Greenwood_ **DATE OF BURIAL** _Oct 25 1918_

15. FILED ___ _Max C Starkeoff_

20. UNDERTAKER _W. C. Gordon_ **ADDRESS** _Harry Morgan_

MISSOURI STATE BOARD OF HEALTH
BUREAU OF VITAL STATISTICS
CERTIFICATE OF DEATH

Do not use this space.

25199

73°

File No.

Registered No. 7621

1. PLACE OF DEATH

County

Township

Registration District No.

Primary Registration District No. 1803

City *St. Louis* (No. *In Quarry, Montour & Atlantic St.*) (Ward)

2. FULL NAME *Elmer Anderson*

(a) Residence. No. *2626 Papin* St., *7* Ward. (If nonresident give city or town and State)
(Usual place of abode)

Length of residence in city or town where death occurred ___ yrs. ___ mos. ___ da. How long in U.S., if of foreign birth? ___ yrs. ___ mos. ___ da.

PERSONAL AND STATISTICAL PARTICULARS	MEDICAL CERTIFICATE OF DEATH

3. SEX *Male* | **4. COLOR OR RACE** *Colored* | **5. SINGLE, MARRIED, WIDOWED OR DIVORCED** (write the word) *Single*

16. DATE OF DEATH (MONTH, DAY AND YEAR) *8/6* 19*25*

17.

5A. IF MARRIED, WIDOWED, OR DIVORCED
HUSBAND of
(OR) WIFE of

I HEREBY CERTIFY, That I attended deceased from ___ to ___ 19___

That I last saw h___ alive on ___ 19___, and that death occurred, on the date stated above, at 2 or ___ m.

6. DATE OF BIRTH (MONTH, DAY AND YEAR) *Dec 13, 1907*

THE CAUSE OF DEATH was as follows:

Drowning
Manner of same not
ascertainable

7. AGE | YEARS *17* | MONTHS *7* | DAYS *24* | If LESS than 1 day, ___ hrs. or ___ min.

(duration) ___ yrs. ___ mos. ___ da.

8. OCCUPATION OF DECEASED
(a) Trade, profession, or particular kind of work *Schoolboy*
(b) General nature of industry, business, or establishment in which employed (or employer)
(c) Name of employer

CONTRIBUTORY (SECONDARY)

(duration) ___ yrs. ___ mos. ___ da.

18. WHERE WAS DISEASE CONTRACTED
IF NOT AT PLACE OF DEATH

9. BIRTHPLACE (CITY OR TOWN) *Mo.*
(STATE OR COUNTRY)

DID AN OPERATION PRECEDE DEATH? ___ DATE OF ___

10. NAME OF FATHER *Floyd Blanks*

WAS THERE AN AUTOPSY?

WHAT TEST CONFIRMED DIAGNOSIS?

11. BIRTHPLACE OF FATHER (CITY OR TOWN) *Ark.*
(STATE OR COUNTRY)

12. MAIDEN NAME OF MOTHER *Ethel Blanks*

(Signed) *F. W. Fath* M.D.

8/8 19*25* (Address) *Deputy Coroner*

13. BIRTHPLACE OF MOTHER (CITY OR TOWN) *Mo*
(STATE OR COUNTRY)

*State the DISEASE CAUSING DEATH, or in deaths from VIOLENT CAUSES, state (1) MEANS AND NATURE OF INJURY, and (2) whether ACCIDENTAL, SUICIDAL, or HOMICIDAL. (See reverse side for additional space.)

14. INFORMANT *H. Sydnor*
(Address) *2343a Chouteau*

19. PLACE OF BURIAL, CREMATION, OR REMOVAL *Washington Park*

DATE OF BURIAL *8/10* 19*25*

15. *Mar. 8 x 40 10*

20. UNDERTAKER ___ **ADDRESS**

Elmer: Born December 13, 1907

Died: August 8, 1925 (17/18 years old)

Elmer was drowned by a gang of boys who'd learned that Elmer had won some tickets to a sporting event and they wanted them. They surrounded him, beat him and drowned him.

MISSOURI DIVISION OF HEALTH — STANDARD CERTIFICATE OF DEATH

59-041731

STATE FILE NUMBER

FILED VS NOV 20 1959

Registrar's No. 210501

1. PLACE OF DEATH		2. USUAL RESIDENCE (Where deceased lived. If institution: Residence before admission)	
a. COUNTY		a. STATE Missouri b. COUNTY	
b. CITY OR TOWN (If outside corporate limits, give TOWNSHIP only) St. Louis Length of stay in 1b		c. CITY OR TOWN St. Louis Inside Limits Yes ☒ No ☐	
c. FULL NAME OF HOSPITAL OR INSTITUTION (If NOT in hospital, give location) Homer G. Phillips Inside Limits Yes ☒ No ☐		d. STREET ADDRESS (If outside, give location) 3351 Clara Reside on Farm Yes ☒ No ☐	

3. NAME OF DECEASED (Type or print) First Juanita Middle Last Davis	4. DATE OF DEATH Month 11 Day 13 Year 59

| 5. SEX Female | 6. COLOR OR RACE Negro | 7. Married ☐ Widowed ☒ Never Married ☐ Divorced ☐ | 8. DATE OF BIRTH 1/16/16 | 9. AGE (last birthday) 43 | IF UNDER 1 YEAR Months Days | IF UNDER 24 HR Hours Min. |

10a. USUAL OCCUPATION Domestic 10b. KIND OF BUSINESS OR INDUSTRY 11. BIRTHPLACE St. Louis, Mo. 12. CITIZEN OF WHAT COUNTRY U.S.A.

13a. FATHER'S NAME Floyd Anderson 13b. MOTHER'S MAIDEN NAME Ethel Banks 14. NAME OF HUSBAND OR WIFE

15. WAS DECEASED EVER IN U.S. ARMED FORCES? 16. SOCIAL SECURITY NO. 17. INFORMANT Mrs. Queaying Pearson Address 5667 Labadie

18. CAUSE OF DEATH
PART I. DEATH WAS CAUSED BY.
IMMEDIATE CAUSE (a) Epidermoid Carcinoma of Cervix. INTERVAL BETWEEN ONSET AND DEATH Undet.

Conditions, if any, which gave rise to above cause (a), stating the underlying cause last. DUE TO (b) _____ DUE TO (c) _____ 171x

PART II. OTHER SIGNIFICANT CONDITIONS CONTRIBUTING TO DEATH but not related to the terminal disease condition given in PART I (a)

PART III. If deceased was female was there a pregnancy in last 90 days? ☐ Yes ☒ No ☐ Unknown

19. WAS AUTOPSY PERFORMED? YES ☒ NO ☐

20a. ACCIDENT ☐ SUICIDE ☐ HOMICIDE ☐ 20b. DESCRIBE HOW INJURY OCCURRED.

20c. TIME OF INJURY Hour a.m. p.m. Month, Day, Year

20d. INJURY OCCURRED WHILE AT WORK ☐ NOT WHILE AT WORK ☐ 20e. PLACE OF INJURY 20f. CITY, TOWN, OR LOCATION COUNTY STATE

21. I attended the deceased from 11-2-59 to 11-13-59 and last saw X alive on 11-13-59
Death occurred at 7:10 a.m. on the date stated above, and to the best of my knowledge, from the causes stated.

22a. SIGNATURE Wm Smiley M.D. (Degree or title) 22b. ADDRESS 2601 N. Whittier 22c. DATE SIGNED 11-13-59

23a. BURIAL, CREMATION, REMOVAL (Specify) Burial 23b. DATE 11/16/59 23c. NAME OF CEMETERY OR CREMATORY Mount Olive 23d. LOCATION St. Louis County, Mo.

24. FUNERAL DIRECTOR Gordon-English ADDRESS 1123 N. Taylor 25. DATE REC'D BY LOCAL REG. NOV 14 1959 26. REGISTRAR'S SIGNATURE Heard Smith M.D.

(Licensed Embalmer's Statement on Reverse Side)

Irma: Born May 8, 1911 Died: February 26, 2006

My grandmother Juanita died November 13, 1959 and was buried next to my great-grandmother.

Juanita Anderson

Birth: 16 Jan 1916

Death: 13 Nov 1959 (aged 43)

Burial: Mount Olive Catholic Cemetery

Lemay, St. Louis County, Missouri, USA

Memorial ID: 47774335

Floyd Anderson Birth: July 15, 1887

Floyd Jr. died on October 23, 1918 from Influenza. After Floyd, Jr. died, Ethel began a relationship with another Chinese man also named Ah Sing, who hadn't changed his name. Ah was born abt 1869. Ethel was of African heritage therefore, could not marry outside her ethnicity. It was the 1920/1930's. However, Ethel and Ah lived and raised their two children (Que Ye and Louis) together. It was primarily a family unit, despite the government's rejection of interracial marriages.

Louis Sung Sing Born: March 29. 1922 Died: January 31, 1914 Que Ye Sing Born: 1920

Aunt Que

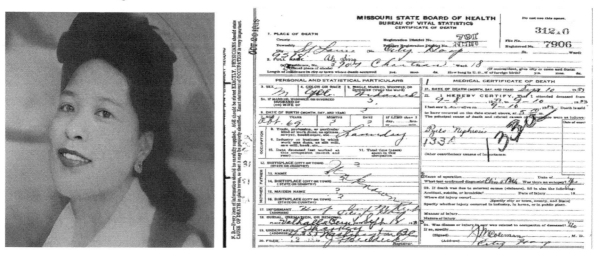

<u>U.S., World War II Draft Cards Young Men, 1940-1947</u> for Louis Sing

REGISTRATION CARD—(Men born on or after January 1, 1922 and on or before June 30, 1924)

SERIAL NUMBER	1. NAME (Print)	ORDER NUMBER
N 50	Louis Sing	11922

2. PLACE OF RESIDENCE (Print)

1123 & S. Montrose   St. Louis, Mo.

[THE PLACE OF RESIDENCE GIVEN ON THE LINE ABOVE WILL DETERMINE LOCAL BOARD JURISDICTION; LINE 2 OF REGISTRATION CERTIFICATE WILL BE IDENTICAL]

3. MAILING ADDRESS   same

4. TELEPHONE   none

5. AGE IN YEARS   20

6. PLACE OF BIRTH   St. Louis

DATE OF BIRTH   March 29, 1922   Mo.

7. NAME AND ADDRESS OF PERSON WHO WILL ALWAYS KNOW YOUR ADDRESS
Ethel Anderson   1123 St. Louis

8. EMPLOYER'S NAME AND ADDRESS
Greengard Drug Co. Clayton, Mo.

9. PLACE OF EMPLOYMENT OR BUSINESS
Clayton, Mo.

I AFFIRM THAT I HAVE VERIFIED ABOVE ANSWERS AND THAT THEY ARE TRUE.

D. S. S. Form 1 (Revised 6-1-42)   (over)   Louis Sing
(Registrant's signature)

Uncle Sung

Because Mom-Mo had children by Chinese men, the majority of them were of light skinned. Back in the 30's and 40's, bright was right. Some lighter people thought they were superior than the others and refused to co-exist with darker skinned people.

My grandmother Juanita married Emmanuel Davis Sr. (Jockko). Their union produced 3 children.

Emmanuel Jr. (My father)

Born: March 16, 1935   Died: July 25, 2016

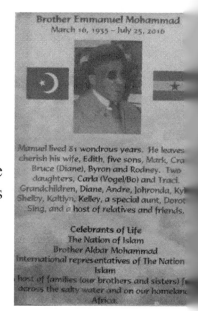

(My father is laid to rest in the motherland) Ghana, Africa) @ his home

Jaqueline   Born: 1937   Died: Unknown

Michael   Born: 1946   Died: 2016

My father's father name was Emmanuel Davis Sr. (nickname: Jockko), born approx. 1915. Word is he was a number's runner however; census papers dictate he was an elevator operator. Jockko married my grandmother Juanita.

Aunt Dorothy and Uncle Sung

When Mom-Mo's children were older and married, the entire family gathered their earnings and purchased a home on the Southside of Saint Louis. Although it was a small home, they managed to live comfortably. When Mom-Mo's off springs began having additional children the home became too small so they sold the home and purchased individual homes. My Uncle Louis Sung and his wife Dorothy agreed to have MomMo live with them.

My grandmother moved on the west side of Saint Louis with her 3 children. The remaining off springs either purchased homes or rented apartments. When my grandmother Juanita died, my Aunt Que assured her sister she would take Michael into her home and raise him like she would her own. It only took about 6-8 months before Michael began living with us on Labadie, directly across the street from Aunt Que.

My father was the darker of the three children. He was caught up in the skin game then and, I think he didn't know where he belonged as a child. But boy, did he find out as he grew into his own. He ended up being a walking African American historian. He became a devout Muslim and read and carried the Holy Karan daily. He knew our (African) history and the Caucasian history and was point on in his discussions with everyone he'd speak with.

My father and mother, (Manuel and Edythe Louis Wynn) married one month after I was born in 1959. They had already had my brother Mark in April of 1958. They were married at St. Henry's Church. Some of my father's family members didn't approve of him marrying my mother because she was dark-skinned and accused her that my brother Mark was not my father's son because he was too dark-skinned. Mark looks exactly like my father, i.e., high cheek bones and slanted eyes.
Mark was simply dark-skinned.

My father Manuel

My mother Edith

My brother Mark

Aunt Que's daughter Veronica also married a dark-skinned person, who was not accepted either. She got divorced and married "light". At one point, Aunt Que asked my mother to accompany her to several juke joints to "monitor his movements". My mother wasn't have it. She knew they disapproved of her and she held nothing back. She told her absolutely not. My mother was a real woman who didn't hold her tongue for anything or nobody. If anyone dared to come inside her lane, she would light you a new asshole. She was not subservient to no one but God. Everyone knew not to cross her.

My father's sister, Jackie married a military man and had 7 children. They were not all by the same man. Jackie always had issues. On one occasion, when her husband was away in the military, she left them alone in the apartment. They had to fend for themselves. I believe the oldest was around 8 or 9 years old at the time. After a few days, neighbors noticed Jackie was never around with any of the children and called Child Welfare. Child Welfare came and took the children away. My father contacted the children's father(s), who came and retrieved their respective children. Prior to her marriage and having children, Jackie was known to have various hair color changes, sometimes daily, and walk the streets. She was never on drugs, she simply had issues. I don't think anybody knew how to help her so, they just let her be. She even had a poodle who she would also color its hair the same as her hair color. Jackie was just different. Later on, about 40 years later, Jackie came to visit her family. My father took myself and my sister over to see her. She first rubbed our hair to see if we had "Black kinky" or "Straight" hair. Immediately, being our mother's children, my sister Traci pushed her hand away and said, "Yeah, we have black, kinky hair and we love it!"

Me	My sister Traci

My mother's parents were Obadiah and Mary Louise Wynn.

Obadiah William Wynn   Born: 9-18-1916   Died: 12-24-1979   (63 years) (Born in Mississippi)

Mary Louise Maddox   Born: 9-2-1918   Died: 1991
(Born in Tillar, Arkansas)

My grandfather, Obadiah's parents were John, born: 1879 (Mississippi), died: 1975 and Rena, born: 1891 (Mississippi), died: 1952. John and Rena, (My great-grandparents) produced 7 children; Letha, Rosella, John Jr., Nannie, Theopplus, Dorothy and Obadiah.

Letha	Born: 1906 (Mississippi)	Died: Unknown
Rosella	Born: 1906 ((Mississippi)	Died: Unknown
John Jr.	Born: 1911	Died: Unknown
Nannie	Born: 1912	Died: 1933
Theopplus	Born: 1913	Died: 1975
Dorothy	Born: 1914	Died: Unknown
Obadiah	Born: 1916	Died: 1979

My great-great grandparents were named Charles and Ella Wynn. They produced 8 children; Albert, Rose Bud, Asa, Bevy, Wolsey, Lelia, Seanie and John.

Charles Wynn	Born: 1848 (Mississippi)	Died: 1922
Ella Wynn	Born: 1858	Died: 1927

My grandmother (momma's mother), Mary Louise was born on September 2, 1928 in Tillar Arkansas to Boss and Cora M (Brooks) Maddox.

Boss Maddox: Born: 1895   Died: June, 1984 (90 years old)

Marry (Brooks)   Born: 1895 Tillar, Arkansas   Died: 1954

Boss and Cora married on November 29, 1917.

MARRIAGE LICENSE

(Coupon to be Detached by County Clerk and Forwarded to State Registrar Vital Statistics, State Capitol)

State of Arkansas

Desha

Boss Maddox .... of ...Tillar

f ...Drew .... State of ...Arkansas

...22 .... Nationality ....Negro .... and

Cora Brooks .... of ...Tillar

f ...Drew .... State of ...Arkansas

...22 .... Nationality ....Negro

12th day of November 19 17.

County Clerk

Deputy County Clerk

Boss married Savanah after Cora died.

Boss and Cora produced 1 child, my grandmother Mary Louise Maddox.
My grandparents Obadiah and Mary Louise married and produced 9 children.
Carl, Marva, Edith, Obadiah Jr. Janice, Harold, Darryl, Roslyn and Gregory

Obadiah Sr. had a decent job during the 50's, 60's and 70's, working at the Post Office. My grandmother was a housewife and eventually began working out of her home doing neighborhood women's hair from her kitchen. My grandfather would bring his check home and give it to my grandmother to take care of the home and bills.

My mother and Marva both attended Buder Community Center, where they learned how to sew and make clothes. They both obtained employment at a hospital,

Obadiah Jr., Harold and Daryl all joined the armed forces. Both my mother and Marva got married. Their sister, Janice obtained employment and an apartment. My youngest Aunt, Roslyn and Uncle Gregory were children during this time.

Wynn Family
Reunion

My mother and father had Mark and I, got married and moved into an apartment. They had 5 more children. Craig, Bruce, Byron, Traci and Rodney.

My father had previously spent some time in the Navy and was able to get a job working at McDonnell Doughlas Aircraft. He was definitely a character from another world. As a youngster, he was the kid who wasn't afraid to try anything. On his bicycle, he would pop willies going fast up and down the streets. He also attended Buder Community Center and learned how to swim, skate and fight. He was a boxer in the Navy and a "floor boy" at Steinberg Skating Ring. He spotted my mother

and fell in love. Rumor has it that all he would need to do is give my grandmother money to date her 16-year-old daughter, my momma. We lived at 5658 Labadie. Our telephone number was EV9-2908. How I can remember that blows my mind. At the time, both my uncles, Harold and Michael were living with us. It was a two-bedroom apartment. At one time, my Aunt Marva also stayed with us while her husband, Uncle James completed college. She had a daughter, Lisa.

Uncle Harold had joined the Navy and got married to Doris. He made a successful career and lived a comfortable life, traveling worldwide and experiencing various cultures. My father's brother, Uncle Michael had also joined the Navy and was comfortable with his duties and status. He was honorably discharged. He became a Scuba Diver. Life sometimes deals you a hand you have no idea where it comes from. Michael was living in Oakland, California and as far as we thought was doing well as a Scuba Diver. After several years being missing in action and no communication whatsoever, Michael showed up on our doorstep with his girlfriend looking like Huggy Bear from the movie "Imma Get You Sucka", just country. Anyway, my mother welcomed them in and began reminiscing. My mother sensed something was happening when she noticed Uncle Michael carrying a large duffle bag. When she asked about it, Michael opened it up and a lot of money flowed out. Momma's eyes lit up and immediately knew what Michael was up to. She screamed at him and told him to put that shit back into the bag and get the hell out of her house. He had become a drug dealer. Michael went back to California and was missing in action for at least the next 15 years. He had been incarcerated. My father, husband and brother Rodney drove all the way to California when he was released and brought him home. My father got him an apartment and set him up with a job, driving a cab for him.

When my brother Rodney was approximately 6 years old, we moved to a community named Laclede Town. Jerry Berger was the mastermind behind Laclede Town. My father and Jerry immediately became friends when they met. Jerry offered my father a job, Manager of Community Affairs. Laclede Town was far from the neighborhood we'd just left on Labadie. During that time, Labadie was a community within the block. Neighbors knew neighbors and often gathered together for card parties, picnics, etc. The only difference was that Laclede Town was much larger and contained people of all colors, backgrounds, ethnicities, and cultures. We hit the jackpot…Utopia.

We lived in a 4-bedroom apartment. Our utopia had a community center, tennis court, baseball field, 5 swimming pools and amphitheaters. On any given Saturday and after a Khory League baseball game, adults could be found listening to poetry, jazz and/or having discussions on the state of the government, world events, religious beliefs, The Black Panther Party, and a host of other important happenings in the neighborhood and around the world.

There were doctors, lawyers, football and baseball players, comedians, musicians, beauticians, librarians, pastors, etc. A mixture of high and low incomes were living in Utopia. Race, religious beliefs, income, nothing mattered but the comradery our piece of paradise had for one another. Laclede Town was a planet of its own. There were parades, football games, talent shows, parent meetings, school meetings, a neighborhood newspaper, everything.

There was a dedicated mother's group who would oversee every aspect of living in our world.

They would attend school meetings, board meetings, church meetings, sports meetings and everything in between. Children knew not to act like fools because we never knew who was watching, and we certainly did not want to get tapped. Parents had the right to tap you upside your head if you were caught being naughty. They would contact your parents and let them know of your mischievousness. When you got home you would be reprimanded by your parents' big time. Parenting was embedded in the adults within Laclede Town. All parents were our parents too. You dared not be immoral to anyone, period.

Lisa

My Aunt Marva and Uncle James lived around the corner from us, which made an awesome experience for me. Although I had a younger sister, Traci, I was closer in age to Lisa.

Lisa and I have a relationship to this day where one knows what the other is thinking and says it before the other. We are definitely more than cousins. There was a couple of neighborhood bars where adults would meet to play dominoes, listen to poetry, jazz and "shoot the breeze". Great notables would live in Laclede Town and visit Laclede Town. Dick Gregory had gone to Sumner Highschool and often visit just to hang out. Great artists such as Shirley Lefore, Oliver Lake, Marham (Akon's father), Michael Landon (Ponderosa television show), his aunt owned the local store and a restaurant, Stokely Carmichael and a host of others. Jerry Berger was adamant that there should be equal opportunity for low-income people to live in Laclede Town as well as high-income tenants. We were family no matter what.

Jerry was previously a DJ and almost always had an after-party in his penthouse. Mick Jagger, Fleetwood Mac, Stevie Nicks, and just about everyone performing at the Arena came to Jerry's for the after-party. I worked inside the main office where they would have to come with Jerry to access the Elevator to the penthouse. I would sometimes be given tickets for the shows. Whenever I would miss the bus to come home from School and report to work, it would be Floyd the guard who'd pick me up from School in either Jerry's Roll Royce or Bentley. Southwest High School students didn't know what to think about me, who I was, and where I came from. None of their business. I rarely fraternized with any of them. During the summer months when the swimming pools were operable, all 5 would be filled with people enjoying each other's company. When they closed for the day and I was working the evening shift at the main office as the receptionist, my siblings and/or friends would call me to let me know they would be hopping the fence and having a swimming party. They knew that all they had to do was call and let me know that they'd be in the pools, so when a neighbor/tenant contacted security, I'd receive the call and not send security. Parties would never be loud, rowdy or confrontational. We were family and fun was always had by all.

My father's position as the Manager of Community Affairs was a great fit, he was extremely extrovert and wasn't afraid of confrontation. He was able to defuse any type of disagreement among adults and/or children. When he spoke, you listened. My father was definitely instrumental in all indoor and outdoor activities for the community. He created a football and baseball organization for all ages. A Community Center was erected with a tennis court and various celebrations were had throughout the year.

My father was known and loved by everyone. He held the reins within the community. Jerry often asked and followed my father's directions as to the needs of the community. My father solicited everyone who wanted to participate in making our utopia.

Reverend Dudley was the Pastor of Berea Church. He opened the church for several events i.e., sporting events, banquets, talent shows, concerts, etc. He was also seen outside the church and into the community, attending little league football games, taping and commentating the plays. Reverend Dudley was definitely before his time. He understood the plight of people of color and wasn't afraid to march for freedom and attend civil rights meetings. He was the first militant Pastor I'd ever known to take his message to the people outside the church and into the community.

Reverend Dudley would open its' doors for the Summer Program to be held. Teenagers (13 – 15 years old) would have the opportunity to make money while learning how important money was. How to calculate, save and spend earnings responsively.

There were several teenagers who applied and all were accepted into the program. The program had several categories to choose from i.e., boardgames swimming lessons, sports, crafting, dancing, beautification, food/lunch distribution and cleanup.

Alice

For the most part, the teenage boys chose sports or swimming, while the girls applied for crafting, dancing or other activities. Very seldom did anyone choose food/lunch distribution or cleanup, that was too much like the chores we already had at home. So, the adults over the program would perform those duties. One of our friends, Alice was somewhat of a fashionista. Even at the tender age of 13, Alice knew fashion and had already decided that after graduating from high School, she would attend some sort of fashion institution to hone her talent in the fashion world and take it by storm. Well, while everyone was choosing and applying for their area of interest for the summer, Alice chose beautification. Alice didn't know that beautification was a fancy word for cleaning up the grounds of our utopia. So, while everyone pretty much received the job they'd wanted, a few of the teenagers, along with Alice were outside in the scorching heat with their pitch fork, garbage bags, gloves and trash containers, the rest of us were enjoying our job responsibilities.

Reverend Dudley would introduce himself and the adult staff who'd be supervising the Summer Program. The Summer Program lasted 6 weeks. Every Monday through Friday, while most of us began and ended our day with a smile, Alice would come into Berea Church to report to work with a frown on her face. She knew she had chosen the wrong category for work. Alice would see everyone having fun performing their job responsibilities and would be disappointed and sad yet, did not give up. She performed her duties every day. She may not have enjoyed doing her duties, but she understood her assignment and collected her pay every two weeks just like the rest of us.

Although we were separated from our friend during working hours, we always ended up together after work. We would swim, walk around Laclede Town and talk about how our day had gone at work. At every corner, Alice would tell us what trash she had to pick up and place inside the trash bin. Her stories were hilarious.

Mary and yours truly, me

There was a beauty shop near the outskirts of Laclede Town. The hairdressers had completely filled their trash cans to the brim. Alice had to scoop up the hair spilled onto the ground. She stated that there were balls and balls, clumps and clumps of hair all over the ground. Alice decided not to use her pitch fork, thinking it would take too long, so she began scooping the hair balls and clumps with her hands. All of a sudden, she hears soft, faded purring.

Alice didn't think anything of it and continued scooping up the hair. Then the purring began louder and louder. That's when she realized that she was not only grabbing balls and clumps of hair but, also, tugging on kittens, grabbing their hair. She immediately dropped everything, knocked over the trash bins and began running and screaming down the streets.

Laclede Town had activist Percy Green, a militant who climbed the Arch in protest of no people of color being able to obtain work on its' construction. There was Dick Gregory, who graduated from the first black high School in St. Louis, Sumner, who would often visit during jazz concerts and various meetings.

Eric Thomas, an artist by trade and an Art teacher at Sumner High School. He was also the person in Laclede Town who would assist anyone wanting to attend college by completing the necessary application paperwork. The college of choice was Southern University in Louisiana. He also wrote several grants for the community. Laclede Town obtained a community center, Peacock Alley, a tennis court, and money to support several sports teams.

Dudley moved into Laclede Town with her seven children. Four of her children were me and my sibling's age. Mary and I became best friends, Martha and my sister Traci became best friends. John and Willie were my brother's Craig and Bruce's age. They played little league sports together. Martha, Mary, Traci and I are still best friends today.

All of my siblings were extrovert. We couldn't help it. Momma and daddy both were. Our mother, of course was our rock. For this, I am extremely forever grateful and appreciative to both my parents.

My brother Mark was the musician, producer, publisher and organizer of Laclede Town talent shows.

At a very young age, Mark would have the neighborhood children audition for talent shows. He would also create a panel of judges who'd choose which person/groups would make the cut. It was always so many children auditioning that it would be at least 2 weeks before the top 10-15 people/groups who had made the cut would be posted throughout the message boards in town. Children would run after Mark and his panel as they would staple the results onto the message boards. It was truly a sight to see. Some would shout and jump up and down while others would cry because they hadn't been chosen to perform at Peacock Alley, the community center. Mark would rent a tuxedo for the event, and it would often sell out. He would sell tickets and of course perform. He wore all these hats. He was even the MC. Half if not all of Laclede Town children and adults purchased tickets. The center was packed. Anyway, Mark had a group perform...Lisa, me, Byron, and he was the leader. I don't remember what song we performed but, I think it was a Michael Jackson song. We began dancing/singing in front of this huge crowd who looked like WTH are these kids doing. Needless to say, we hadn't perfected the performance. We were so out of step and knew we weren't doing a good job. We could see our friends and family's faces looking sorry for us in the audience. Later we found out that Martha had tilted her head towards my mother and said, "Nookie, I don't think they're going to win". My mother burst out laughing. She undoubtedly agreed.

Crazy ass Mark, the big-time leader of our group, thought it necessary to "save" the performance. So, what does he do? His dumb ass leaves formation and begins his own solo performance. Now, not only is the crowd looking like WTH, me Lisa and Byron are looking at Mark thinking WTH. After losing, we confronted Mark and asked what was he thinking. He told us to shut the hell up and that he was trying to "save" us. As if he alone breakdancing and singing would change the outcome of us losing. It did not.

That night Mark wore his tux to bed. Although we lost, we had a ball. Mark, with his producing, songwriting, newspaper editor, jack-of-all-trades, go-gettin' "crazy ass" launched his musical career @ Peacock Alley that night.

Earnings from his talent shows and group fees would be collected and at the end of the summer, he would take the group on a trip. We had gone to Illinois to see Donna Summer. Mark was before his time. He had great penmanship and created a weekly newsletter that included music and the artists, gossip around town and his personal opinions.

As we became older, my mother obtained a position at a hospital. She assigned Mark "manager" duties over the rest of us to make sure we completed our daily chores. One time he had found a dirty wash cloth in the bathroom and asked us who'd left it in there. None of the six of us acknowledged it. Mark made each of us grab a piece of the wash cloth and carry it to the dirty clothes hamper. He would make us and some of the neighborhood children attend his summer school. Of course, he'd be the principal. After a couple of weeks, he would send

24

written report cards home with us to have our parents sign and remark if they chose so. All of the parents signed the report cards and some even made comments. He was only around 15 years old, when we attended his school.

Even back then parents and children knew the importance of education, even if it was summer. It was fun learning. Mark was also the neighborhood prankster. He would gather us all into the basement and make crank calls to people. Mark would get balloons and have us all fill them with water and wait on the bus stop. When the bus driver opened the door, we all would bomb him and anyone sitting close to the front. One time the bus driver stopped the bus, unbuckled his seat belt and chased us throughout the community. Guess who got caught? Mark. The bus driver asked Mark where he lived and took him home to my parents. Mark got the worst whooping of his life when the bus driver left. We never did that again in fear of the same repercussion.

I would often cook dinner and dessert while our mother and father were at work. On one occasion, I decided to make a chocolate cake for dessert. Mark didn't like that I told all my siblings that although they could eat dinner, I wanted the cake to remain intact until our parents were able to eat dinner and we'd all enjoy dessert together. Mark didn't agree, after being told no one would be able to eat dessert until momma and daddy finished eating dinner, he began beating up the cake. He balled up his fist and started throwing and punching the cake all over the kitchen. He even threw some of the beaten, lopsided cake outdoors on the ground. Mark was somewhat of a spoiled brat.

We had a choice of choosing which swimming pool we'd swim on a daily basis. On a hot, sunny day and after swimming in the largest pool, me, Lisa, and a friend, Claudia, walked down Washington Ave.

| Me | Lisa | Claudia |

Low and behold prostitutes were walking up and down the streets. We were about 11 or 12 and were astonished to see them walk up to cars. Some would get into the cars and some would not. We stood and watched them for about 15 minutes. For some dumb ass reason, we decided to start calling them sluts, whores, "Toot, toot, beat, beat". Where this phrase came from, I couldn't tell you, we just came up with it. All of sudden 3-4 of the prostitutes heard us and started walking towards us. Needless to say, all three of us started running our asses off. Finally, we were back inside Laclede Town and ran into the Security Guards, Ernie and Floyd. They asked us why we were running so fast and out of breath. We huffed and puffed until we got enough air and told them that we had been chased by "Some real live whores". They both fell out laughing. We didn't think it was funny, we were scared as hell they'd catch us and beat the shit out of us.

Marba was the owner of the General Store. She was Michael Landon's aunt. She even named her restaurant "The Ponderosa". Laclede Town's electrical boxes were located outside of the townhomes and apartments, and were easily accessible, the doors were unlocked. The neighborhood children, about 15-20 of us would occasionally go inside the store and situate ourselves next to the items we'd like to have. As soon as the one designated person switched the electric off, all of us grabbed and ran out the door with the items. When everyone was out that person would switch the lights back on. We all would meet up behind Harris Stowe State College and show, open and share what we had stolen. All items were edible except one package. Martha, an eight-year-old had grabbed a box of Kotex. We all laughed and explained to her what the package was and that it was not edible. She started to cry. Everybody gave Martha a little of their treat and she was happy. Later on, Mary told me that Dudley, Martha's mother took her back to the store with the box of Kotex and apologized to Marba.

Because of the men in the community, there were plenty of sports to learn, play and have fun. My brothers Craig, Bruce and Rodney all played baseball and football.

 Craig   Bruce

Byron   Rodney

My brother Byron was into tennis. One of the coaches, Eric Thomas, assisted any and everyone who wanted to attend college. Craig, Bruce and Rodney attended Southern University.

Traci

My sister Traci also attended Southern. Craig played baseball and was a natural, he was a pitcher. Bruce played football; his position was kicker. He was also a natural. Bruce was severely injured and was unable to continue playing so, he became somewhat of an employee for the team. Craig was already a star pitcher and even had scouts coming to see him. He somehow got the notion that he was so good that he no longer had to attend classes to play ball. He eventually joined the marines. Byron joined the Army and was discharged. Even before Traci attended Southern University, she was in a high school program where she'd work for the Metropolitan Sewer District. After a couple of years in college, Traci decided to return home and continue working at MSD for the next 30 years. Rodney came home and worked at General Electric and GM Motor Company. Craig received an honorable discharge and obtained various government jobs. Byron secured a manufacturing position. Mark quit high School, got his GED, and began working as a Counselor for Sanford-Brown Institute, an institution that trained people to get a job in their desired field. Mark eventually moved to New Orleans. Luckily, he returned back home right before Katrina hit. He then obtained a position at Washington University as a coder.

We had an older friend named Janelle who had attended and graduated from Cosmetology School and became a Beautician. I scheduled an appointment with her to get my hair done. After arriving at Janelle's apartment, she asked me to go upstairs and retrieve a hair conditioner she had developed and swore it would repair damaged hair. I proceeded to go upstairs into her bathroom to get the jar she'd asked me to retrieve. I sat down and Janelle proceeded to wash my hair with her newly developed hair shampoo and conditioner. All of a sudden, the air began reeking of a foul odor. We didn't know what the smell was coming from and Janelle assured me that it wasn't the concoction she'd developed. The odor began to overcome the entire apartment. I stopped Janelle from washing my hair and questioned her. She showed me the shampoo and conditioner jar she'd asked me to retrieve. Guess what? That odor was indeed coming from that jar and now it was embedded in my scalp. She had directed me to get the wrong jar. The jar she was using to wash and condition my hair was another concoction she had created from egg shells, water and vinegar to grow her plants. I nearly fell out of the chair. Janelle apologized and retrieved the correct jar and finished my hair. Needless to say, I never made another appointment with that nutcase.

Janelle

Laclede Town had become such a success, a utopia, that management decided to create phases. Phase I would be called "Breakthrough" and Phase II would be called "Laclede East". Laclede Town began deteriorating within approximately 5-7 years of the phases being operable. It was too much for Jerry to manage. He had new management who did not support the "Utopia" idea. Management began allowing anyone into our community. The city had torn down several low-income housing projects, most of those families relocated to into Laclede Town. The original tenants began leaving. Drugs, fights, confrontations, etc. had infiltrated our village. Laclede Town was no longer our utopia.

I was still working at Laclede Town as the evening shift receptionist and attending Harris Stowe College, majoring in Computer Science. I met a young lady by the name of Sallie Gooch. Gooch and I meshed immediately. She had a car and we went everywhere together. Instead of attending classes, we'd spend the majority of our time in the Annex playing cards, playing backgammon, and listening to the jukebox. "Groovy People" by Lou Rawls was one of our favorites. Being young and aware of healthy living styles, I ate boiled eggs, fruits, and vegetables. I weighed approximately 102 pounds. You couldn't tell me I wasn't the shit. Since I lived in "Breakthrough", I was able to walk to Harris. On one occasion while walking to Harris, this guy approached me and asked if he could have a bite of my boiled egg. Without lifting my head to see who was speaking, I said absolutely not and kept walking. Unbeknownst to me, that guy was the same guy both Gooch and I had a crush on. We had stalked him and knew his every move, where his classes were and even followed him and found out where he lived.

Vogel (Bo)

When Gooch and I did decide to attend classes, we'd meet in the Annex after. Instead of getting something to eat, we would make our daily run to the liquor store. The guy who worked the counter at the store had a crush on me, so I could get anything I wanted for free. While walking to Gooch's car, that guy we had a crush on approached us and asked if he could go with us. We both were elated. Upon arriving at the liquor store, I exited the car to get our daily free drinks. However, the guy, who had introduced himself as Bo, asked that Gooch retrieve the liquor because he wanted to speak with me. I was so happy because at that moment I knew he was interested in me and not Gooch. But there was a problem, Gooch was unable to get the free liquor. Bo offered to pay for it and gave Gooch money to purchase the liquor. Bo and I talked and he asked me out and of course I said yes.

Bo picked me up from my house and we went to Forest Park, sat in the car and talked. We clicked beautifully. At the end of the date, he had the nerve to ask if he could borrow $10.00 from me. I agreed and gave him the $10.00 bill. He pulled out an ink pen and asked that I sign the bill. WTH was going on I thought. We went on about 5-6 more dates. He finally told me he had a question to ask me. I said, "Okay, what is it?" He replied, "Why haven't you asked about the $10.00 you loaned me"? I told him that he must have needed it and that he would return it when possible. He just looked at me confused and said, "I want to show you something" and pulled out a $10.00 bill. He pointed to my signature and said, "I just wanted to see what type of person you are". He was testing me to see if I was a gold digger, although he was nowhere being a millionaire, not even close. I was glad that I had passed the test. This is the guy that we had a crush on, stalked and knew his every move.

After about 8 months Bo and I decided to become exclusive but, there was another problem. We both were dating someone out of town. He was dating someone at college, and I was dating someone in California who was attending pilot training school. We decided to contact them and let them know. Bo drove up to see her and let her know the circumstances. Since there was no way, I was driving to California, I opted to call my boyfriend to end our long-distance relationship. He had the audacity to ask for my cousin Lisa's telephone number, as if she'd be interested in my left overs.

Bo and I became inseparable. By then he had met my immediate family members. He was from Arkansas and had come to Saint Louis via Germany, an honorable discharged veteran. He lived with his uncle and aunt and their 3 children (Uncle Uellis, Aunt Dean, Gwen, Mirchelle and Edward). I didn't get the chance to meet Edward, he died when he was 17 years old. Eventually Gwen and Mirchelle had children. I was nowhere near wanting children of my own so, I was able to bond with their children. Gwen had Maney and Cadace while Mirchelle had Chasity and Cierra. I became very close to all 4 children. They would spend a lot of time with Bo and I going to the parks, picnics, carnivals. I had an exceptional and grateful relationship with them all.

Bo had a large family and they were a close-knit family. Yearly reunions were attended by at least 150 – 200 family members. After exclusively dating for a year, Bo invited me to attend a reunion. Suffice it say, I was apprehensive. When we drove up to his parent's home there were about 40 adults and about 15 children playing in the yard. I was panicking, "What if they don't like me". As soon as I got out of the car I hear, "Carla, Carla, Carla's here" and children running up to me hugging me, almost knocking me down. It was my 4 Saint

Louis connection children i.e., Maney, Candace, Chasity and Cierra. Whew, that took my worries away. Later I found out that the adults appreciated me with or without having my babies run to me. At the time I was afraid of meeting all the adults at once and my babies were my buffer. Just being hugged by each of them reinforced my mind that everything would be just fine. It was. Bo's family were receptive, loving, affectionate and approved of our relationship.

Bo's mother and father,
Darthy and Mossie Bonds

They told me that they had never seen Bo so happy before. His mother and father, affectionately called "Momma Darthy & Daddy Nig" were amazingly down to earth and welcomed me with open arms. The rest of the family also extended warmth and love. I began going every year. I've always loved children and taking care of them. Whenever we attended a reunion. I was the keeper of my precious babies. We'd have an all-day swimming/dance party and end with a pizza party. The hotel manager would always allow me to remain in the pool with the children after closing time. We'd have popcorn, snow cones, ice cream and candy, snacks, etc. Bo would always say I'd spend too much money preparing for the reunion by purchasing games and prizes, but boy, did they love playing and having fun. There was always 10–20 children I would have with me.

I was the prankster and always had the children painting their sleeping adult uncles and cousins' fingernails, putting make up on their faces, only for them to wake up and chase the children for fun. Bo's brother Larry, asked me if I had some gum. I reached inside my purse and gave him 2 Feen-a-mint (constipation) pieces. The next day he woke up complaining to Momma Darthy that he must have eaten some bad food because his stomach was upset. That's when I told him what I had done. I had become so loved, and loved my new family, that I was already known as a prankster and was able to get away with pretty much

31

any and everything as a prank. They all knew it was out of playfulness and love. Momma Darthy and Daddy Nig had 8 children together, Bo, Larry, Diane, Junior, Diane, Ellis, Karry, Faye and Marvin.

Darthy and Mossie Bonds Family Reunion

Daddy Nig had 2 children, Shirley and Thomas. Bo, Larry and Junior joined the Army. Ellis joined the Navy. Karry and Marvin obtained jobs. Diane became a nurse, and Faye married her high school sweetheart. Shirley and Thomas (Dr.) both got married.

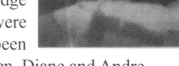

Bo had jury duty and befriended the judge. During communication with the judge, Bo told him we were planning to marry at the courthouse. The judge offered to marry us in his courtroom. We were married on July 10, 1986. Since then, we had been trying to have children. Bo had 2 previous children, Diane and Andre. I wanted my own child. My female organs were not ideal for me to be able to have my own child. Between having fibroid growths and my left ovary removed; it became somewhat obvious it wasn't going to happen for me. We were told that we'd be unable to have children. God's plan didn't mesh with the doctors. We had 2 miscarriages, the first one at 4 months, the 2nd at 5 months. The day I found out that I was pregnant, I went to Macy's and purchased maternity clothes. I was ecstatic. I performed that ritual both times. The third time we became pregnant, I didn't allow myself to actual believe my baby would make it. I wore my

  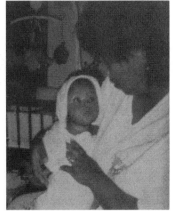

mother's clothes, they were oversized. Guess what happened? God's plan. Shelby Marie Bonds came 3 months early and weighed 1.5 pounds, January 30, 1997.

Shelby remained in the NICU Dept. until April and came home on oxygen. Again, the doctor informed us that Shelby would have difficulties to overcome because she was a preemie. She began receiving SSI checks however, after around the 4 or 5th month of appointments and tests, doctors determine that Shelby did not have any disabilities. Shelby would lead a normal, healthy life.

When She was 13 years old, I felt a lump on her back. She was diagnosed with Scoliosis. I lost it, I thought I'd lose my baby. Shelby received the surgery to correct her Scoliosis/spine. She has since graduated from Fontbonne University with a Bachelor's Degree in Human Services and a Master's Degree in Early Autism Intervention and Sensory Impairment from Lindenwood University.

Shelby's Fontbonne Univ. graduation

Through the years, I found out that my father did not like staying in one job for too long. He got restless and started his own business after leaving Laclede

Town. He later taught me, Bo and my youngest brother Rodney, how to start a cab business. We would meet on Sundays and place whatever money we could into savings. Once we accumulated enough money, we purchased property. Our siblings rented the apartments. Bo and I had already began purchasing rental properties as a couple and had acquired several buildings.

Because of having the opportunity to grow up in our Laclede Town utopia, I've been blessed to have the same group of friends for over 55 years. We are still together. We went to grade school, high School and some of us to college together. I most definitely have an array of playful, serious, pranksters, entertainers, religious, serious, mental and all of the not mentioned characteristics of people in my life who I will be forever grateful to and for.

My cousin Lisa and I grew up living one apartment down from one another. I had originally gone to St. Francis Xavier Catholic School, while Lisa went to Waring Public School. Although separated during school days, we were inseparable after School. The majority of children in Laclede Town attended Waring. Mary, John, Willie and Martha all attended another Catholic School. My siblings and I knew everybody regardless of the school difference because we all lived in Laclede Town. By the time my brother Byron was of school age school tuition began to make a dent in the money jar so, Mark, Carla, Craig and Bruce were all transferred to Waring. That's also where Byron, Traci and Rodney began Kindergarten. The transition was seamless because all of our friends were already known. We no longer had to make the almost 45 minutes' walk to School, it was 5 minutes away and we were able to walk with our friends. I was in the sixth grade and Lisa was in the 5th. Because the mother's group was also deeply participants in our education and attended each and every school meeting and/or event, they practically knew the curriculum and assignments before we knew them and was adamant homework was completed before going outdoors to play. All of us knew to listen, learn and ask questions of our teachers to make sure we understood the work given to us prior to leaving School. That meant that when we got home, we were able to review our notes and complete homework in time to meet each other after.

There were talent shows at Berea Church for adults and children. Pam, Lavel and Artemis, The Meditations were an outstanding teenage group. Lisa, Claudia and myself also performed, along with other teenage groups. It was a mixture of children and adults. You could say we were the opening acts for the real entertainers. Poets, jazz musicians and various artists performed. Needless to say, they were truly the stars and entertainment the audience actually came to see. But our world included everyone, even the children.

Laclede Town had a nemesis… Blumeyer. Blumeyer was also a community however, nowhere near Laclede Town's status. They didn't have a lot of the things that made our utopia a world of its own. Blumeyer was about 30 minutes away from Laclede Town but, it was definitely worlds apart. Some of the Blumeyer children would often trek to utopia to play on various teams within Laclede Town. We met a few friends, Kim Juliette and Sable. There were more boys than girls who made the trek because of the sport teams they were able to participate in. Girls' sports came later during our teenage years however, we did have cheerleading squads.

Of course, the mothers oversaw cheerleading. My mother and Aunt Marva made our skirts and even our pom poms. After tryouts and practicing cheers, the girls who had made the squad had to vote for a captain and co-captain. There were 10 of us who had made the team. I won the captain spot because of 1 vote. It was Lisa's vote that pushed my numbers over. I had voted for myself and it was a tie between Lisa and I being captain and Lisa's vote secured my position. She was Co-Captain. We cheered for the Laclede Town Jets. The Coaches of all of the sporting and cheerleading teams were in it to win it, as if we were actually in the big leagues. They instilled in us hard work, to take everything we did serious with the idea of becoming the best we could be by overcoming our fears. We understood the mission. Our football team even played the championship in the Saint Louis Cardinals football stadium during an actual Cardinals half-time. Paula, Claudia's sister, had taught us cheers and how to cheer, with enthusiasm and purpose. We thought we had made the big time and were actually NFL players and cheerleaders.

During the summer, Blumeyer children would walk over and terrorize some of us. Boys would like girls and chase us periodically and catch us. We never knew what their intentions were but, by the time they were descending upon us, our Laclede Town protectors had come to our rescue. One time the Blumeyer boys had come over and pricked the thorns off bushes and were chasing us to stick us. Lisa and I ran towards my father's car. The plan was that I would get in the back seat while Lisa would get in the front. Well, the simple plan didn't work. When I got in the back of the car, Lisa swiftly closed the door, slamming the door on my hand. She had closed the door too quickly and my hand was stuck in the damn door. I screamed so loud! screaming for her to open the door. That damn door was hurting my hand. The plan had not worked, Lisa got out, opened the door and we both began running away again. When they caught one of us, the rest of us would stop running away and run towards the girl(s) they'd caught. An argument would develop. They said, "Don't you know we're from Blumeyer?" and we will beat you down. Well, Patrice was one of the girls they had caught and immediately came back with "We don't give a damn if you're from Oscar Meyer". ALL of us, including our chasers fell out laughing. From that moment on, we had additional brothers/protectors.

Lisa and I were two peas in a pod. When one of us were on our monthly cycle, the other would bring soup and crackers to the other. We taught ourselves how to play backgammon and experimented in making Carmel popcorn. My mother didn't drive at the time so, we would go shopping with Aunt Marva and Lisa often. We had gone to Ventures and while my mother and Marva would be together shopping, Lisa and I would be shopping. Well, Lisa and I noticed some jewelry we loved and took it upon ourselves to remove the items and place them inside our pockets. We continued as if we had done nothing wrong. As my mother, Marva, me and Lisa began walking out of the store, a security guard approached us and told our mothers what we had done. They took us in the back of the store in an office. That scared the shit out of us, we thought we were going to jail. Our mothers were so embarrassed from what their daughters had done that we were on punishment the entire summer. On the last day of summer Lisa and I were able to attend the last Khory League baseball game. As we walked towards the baseball field, a friend of ours, Davey (Sleepy) turned around and noticed us. He then turned back around towards the spectators and yelled out, "Everybody hold their purses, here come the thieves". Lisa and I was so embarrassed but, we kept walking. There was no way we were going back; we were too happy to be out. We sucked it up, watched all the stares and glares from the spectators and took a seat and watched the rest of the game. Inside we wanted to beat the shit out of Sleepy. Sleepy was an intelligent young boy who was a questionable type of boy. He liked to read and was able to hold deep conversations with adults. He was a young walking dictionary. While working at Laclede Town and walking home from work drinking wine that Jerry Berger had snuck to me, Sleepy asked me what I was drinking. When I told him, he asked if he could taste it. I obliged and gave him my cup to take a sip. Evidently, he didn't like it because he immediately spit it out all over me. I was pissed off at him for about a week. Karma came to bite Sleepy in his ass sometime later.

 Sleepy  Kevin

Kevin, Sleepy and I would often go out to the clubs together. On one occasion, Sleepy was slow dancing on the floor with a woman who he thought was gorgeous, and was all over the woman. Kissing and grabbing her butt, rolling and pumping. He was out of control. Little did he know, it was a man dressed as a woman. It was so obvious to Kevin and I. As soon as the music stopped, Sleepy came over to us looking as if he had found his wife, he was elated to let us know that, he not only got his groove on with this woman but, also her telephone number. Kevin and I immediately broke out into laughter. Sleepy had a look on his face as though as to say, "What the hell is so funny?" Finally, Kevin told him that it was a man he was doing all that damn bumping and grinding with, not a woman. Sleepy was so mad at us for not letting him know before he had asked the woman to dance. But, by the time we got back to the table from ordering drinks, his ass was already up on the floor. We weren't going to embarrass Sleepy nor his dance partner. It was what it was.

I would often receive bottles of Blue Nun when Jerry had after parties and shared with friends at Harry's house. Harry lived in Grand Forest, located directly across the street from Breakthrough. By then we had formed an everyday group of friends. We were teenagers by then. Our group of friends knew that the guy who worked at the liquor store had a crush on me and I was able to retrieve liquor without having to pay for it. Me, Lisa and Alice would walk to the liquor store and get our liquor, go over to my house and drink. One day, Harry called and said that he Michael, James and Calvin were hanging over his house and asked if we had any liquor.

Our childhood/teenager
protectors/brothers....
Harry, Kelvin, Michael and
James

We said yes. He asked us to come on over and bring the liquor, we'd play cards and listen to music. What Harry and the guys didn't know was that we had already drank all of the liquor but, wanted to play cards and listen to music so, we filled the empty bottles with water and walked over to Harry's. They drank all the liquor and started acting like they were drunk. It was hilarious to see them, thinking they were drunk. We knew there was not a drop of liquor in the bottles. We still danced and played cards and had a ball "Cuttin' up".

Lisa was the first of us who actually had a boyfriend. His name was Burnell. Burnell was James' friend, they both attended Vashon High School. One night Lisa and Burnell was down in her basement making out and Mark tip toed down the basement steps watching them kissing. Eventually, Mark started laughing so hard at them and ran back up the steps. Lisa had always wanted a body of a curvaceous women however, during her teenage years, she had a small petite frame. She wanted more, and what Lisa wants, Lisa gets. She wanted to be sexy. She invited a friend over to swim. She purchased a beautiful one-piece black swim suit. It didn't fit too well in the breast area so, what did she do? Lisa stuffed the breast part of the swim suit. During her and her friend's sexy swim, some type of substance began to surface. Her friend questioned what could that have been. Needless to say, Lisa never faltered, she made up some type of story and the sexy swim date continued.

We would often be in each other's basement when it was too cold or dark outside. On most occasions, it would be our basement the gang would hand out in. Mark was always into music so everybody knew we could dance and have fun. We had friends, Vicki and Alice, sisters, who were definitely extroverts. Alice could've easily been a comedian and Vicki an actress. Alice could also sing; she was beautiful and a had an aura that exhumed fun and friendliness. She had a sharp tongue too. She would spit out a comeback if you dared to make a derogatory statement to her or about her. Whenever we didn't have anything to do, we'd create our own fun.

One of my best friends, Karl Clark moved to Breakthrough. He had a brother, Leonard and a sister, Toni. Leonard was the quiet type and played baseball while Karl was the extrovert. They had a sister Toni, whose was a bit older than the rest of us and had already established a group of friends outside of Laclede Town. She eventually would marry James' older brother Dwight. On one occasion Alice and I

went with Karl to the mall just Karl Leonard Toni to have something to do. Once there, we began our normal antics. Alice noticed a book store and we all decided to go look at books. Well, once we

Karl   Leonard   Toni

were done viewing books, Alice, all of sudden screams, "Books, books, I haven't read a book in a long as time" and started throwing books left and right. Of course, Karl and I looked at one another knowing Alice was in her playful mood, so, we joined her in picking up and throwing books all over that store. Needless to say, mall security ran us out of the store. Vicki had a memory out of this world. She would act out Pam Grier roles from movies, crawling all over the floor saying the exact lines of each character in the movie. Not only 1 or 2 movies, all of the movies we attended, Vicki was able to act them out for us. She made the roles hilarious. Karl was another prankster and is still a prankster to this day. He looked and thought he was one of

Yolonda

the best-looking teenagers ever. He refused to have what he thought ugly girls riding in his front seat because he didn't want anyone to think that was his girlfriend. One time we headed over the bridge to one of Karl's friends 's house. Karl had started smoking weed, which I rarely did and passed me the joint. We were drinking and now smoking weed. As we were getting into the car there was an explosion somewhere in East St. Louis. I was so high off of the liquor and smoking weed I thought I'd seen a UFO and aliens coming out of it. I immediately began screaming and crying and very quickly crawled underneath the car. Needless to say, crazy ass Karl just stood there laughing his ass off at me asking me what the hell was I doing.

Yolonda would sometimes accompany us to parties but she felt more comfortable in smaller settings. She was fun to be around and always kind and gentle with everyone. 'Yolonda worked at Famous-Barr. She and I gave a neighborhood Halloween party for children 5–13 years old.

We made flyers and stapled them throughout Laclede Town on the message boards. Yolonda was able to use her discount for toys, prizes and games.

Floyd, the security guard's daughters attended. He had a daughter who was 14 years old and was not able to attend because of her age. She ran home crying to her father. Floyd came over to the house and asked if we'd let her participate in the festivities. Of course, we said yes. The only reason we cut the age off at 14 is because we didn't think a 14-year-old would have fun. Yolonda and I were so happy that the party was a success. Our mother's had taught us to do what we could to make children happy.

By the time we started going to parties, there were two fraternities that would let us know when they were having a party. They knew us from either living in Laclede Town and playing on one of many sport teams, attending high School with us or, simply knowing 1 or 2 of us. It was somewhat of a battle between the Kappa's and the Q's to decide which party we would attend. The majority of Laclede Town teenagers attended Southwest High School although we had some attending McKinley (Yolonda), Beaumont (Dell) and Sumner (Craig, Bruce, Michael P., Mike F., Curt and Cam). I didn't like Southwest; we were one of the first waves of African Americans attending Southwest and some of the instructors were prejudice as hell. I did make friends with some students. We focused on partying a lot. We were asked to attend a house party. Upon arrival everybody was asked to pay $5.00 to enter. Of course, we asked why and was told that the guy giving the party needed money to purchase new furniture. I told him "Then your ass should go to Rent-A-Center". Needless to say, we went back home and had our own party.

During one of many of the fraternity parties we attended, we were asked to attend an "After Party". They would ask us to wait on them to make sure the place was clean and locked down before they could leave. Alice, Lisa and I sat at a table and watched the maintenance crew come out with a mop, bucket and a couple of sweepers. The maintenance crew were taking so long that we decided to have fun by giving them a talent show. Alice wrung the mop out and began singing a Diana Ross song. What did Lisa and I do? We grabbed the brooms and became her backup singers. The maintenance crew looked at one another, turned and looked at us. We thought they were gonna curse us out big time. They simply paused, grabbed chairs, sat, and watched the show. The frat boys also joined the maintenance crew for the show. All three of us, Lisa, Alice, and I, were always spontaneous and goofy. If we wanted to have fun by doing silly things, we'd do it, no matter what anybody thought. We were the go-to girls for laughter and fun.

As we became young adults and went our separate ways, we always found ourselves together where we'd started. Bo and I were married and had Shelby. Because we all loved music and who doesn't, I'd have yearly BET Parties. I'd have the rope and red carpet, take pictures, give everyone their VIP badges and escort them to the table to complete their BET form. I'd download the list of all categories and prospects. Guests would complete and turn them into to Traci. Traci would keep track of who guessed the correct winner. Awards would be given to the winner. Mark was the commentator, Byron barbecued, I'd make spaghetti and potato salad. Guests would bring dessert. The meat would be ordered. We'd have Halloween, birthday and holiday parties with family and friends.

2016 BET Celebration

2023 Yard Party

Ava's Birthday Party

As we got older, as life goes, some friends were called home earlier than expected. Only God/Allah knows our path on this planet. After attending homegoing celebrations, repasses, etc., we would often meet at our house to eat, drink and reminisce, enjoying each other's company.

My father retired and decided to move to Ghana and build a home, as he would say, "I want my children and grandchildren to have a place to come visit and/or live in the Motherland". The house sits up a hill where beautiful views of the ocean could easily be seen. Banana trees are at arm's length. The villagers all knew, love and respected my father. Daddy was a Muslim and studied under the Honorable Louis Farrakhan. Brother Akbar was the minister's right-hand man stationed in Saint Louis. Bo and I would often go to the Mosque to learn the teachings with my father. My father would sometimes accompany Brother Akbar to Ghana where one of many Mosques were located. Daddy fell in love with the Motherland. Of course, he asked my mother to uproot the family and move to Ghana. Being a rock, solid, grounded person, my mother wasn't having it. She told him that she and her children were not being uprooted to enter an unknown situation. My father would return at least one year to visit. My brother Rodney is also a Muslim and was with my father every step of the way. My father was called home to Allah however, Rodney often visits and ensures the house is in order. Rodney is now the owner and knows a few people in Ghana that often check on the house. Our father's remains are also in Ghana, he had already told us that when Allah calls him home, not to bring his body back to the United States. He knew its history, extremely well and refused to be laid to rest in this devilish country. He was 81 years old.

The home our father built
in Accra Ghana

Daddy's Celebration

My mother retired after receiving knee cap surgeries on both knees. Bo and I purchased 2 townhouses next to each other. This is where my mother and father lived. Eventually, my momma had to receive Dialysis three times a week. She didn't want to be placed on a list to receive a kidney and she didn't want any of us donating one. She was also a spiritual person. She accepted the path that God gave her and was grateful she could see all of her children grow into adulthood and do well. They both were able to meet and spend time with their grandchildren.

Mark was also on dialysis but didn't really want to have to go thru the process. He also had diabetes. My mother pleaded with Mark to have a kidney operation and be able to get dialysis. He was afraid, however, and decided to do it for my mother's sake. Mark would often be depressed with his health and not attend treatments. Because of this, he was often hospitalized and received dialysis at the hospital. Being on dialysis 3 times a week takes a toll on you physically and mentally. Because my mother had been on dialysis, at least 12 years, her arms often became too weak. She had to have the fistula taken from her arms and placed in her neck. This procedure was done approximately 3 times. The last time the procedure was done, the doctor hit a nerve and caused my momma to have a stroke. She was in the hospital about 3 days. When she came home, I brought her to our house and we took care of her here. While she was recuperating, she was starting to slur her words. Something wasn't right. We took her back to the hospital. During this time, we thought Mark was going to his dialysis appointments. But he wasn't. I don't think Mark thought my mother would recover from the stroke and having to be placed back into the hospital. Momma made it home and had recovered. Mark had stopped going to his appointments. None of us realized it and it was too late. I received a call from the hospital informing me that Mark had transitioned. I begged them not to call my mother and asked that they let me tell her face to face but, to no avail. They had already contacted her. I contacted my siblings and told them to meet at momma's house.

You can imagine how we felt as a family. Both my brother and Craig decided it would be us to go to the hospital to take care of Mark's business matters while the rest of her children remained with her for support. My mother decided to donate his body to the Midwest Transplant Society. Unfortunately, they were unable to use any of Mark's organs however, were able to use his skin for burn victims. I decided not to let my mother read the letter we received as to what part(s) of his body they used. She was okay with the fact that she wanted him to be able to help someone in need. We celebrated Mark's life in an uplifting manner. We made sure to everyone who'd be attending his celebration that our mother wanted a celebration, nothing somber. There were about 200 people who attended.

Mark was definitely into Facebook and had at least one thousand followers. He'd give his takes on music, crime, politics, and everything else. He was adamant about black-on-black crimes not being anyone's fault but our own. The black community. He sparked positive and negative conversations regarding blaming the white man for black-on-black crimes. He would end such conversations by sarcastically saying "It's the White Man's fault". Mark's point of view was always to lay  blame where it should be. Black people are harming one another at alarming rates. Mark also knew of police brutality towards people of color, especially black people however, understood that we can't blame the white man for the Black-on-Black crime in Saint Louis. At Mark's celebration, an old friend, Karl brought a 36-inch cheese cake just for my mother. It read, "It's the white man's fault".

Instantly, it brought a smile on her face because it instantly took her back to Mark's Facebook posts. Karl's special gesture gave her smiles and even a laugh. That gesture seemed to have relaxed momma and made her able to celebrate Mark in the fashion he would've wanted us to. Mark was an avid Sylver's fan, the 1980's singing group and was friends on Facebook with one of the singers. Mark's Facebook page had so many condolences that I decided to blow some up and place them around the hall where his celebration was held. The Sylvers even sent their condolences.

Mark's Celebration

Our beautiful momma was called home/transitioned at the age of 81. Both our mother and Mark are cremated. Neither wanted a funeral, they wanted a celebration and that's exactly what we gave them. Of course, there were tears. We still cry for our father, brother and mother. They are all joined together in Paradise with our ancestors. If I don't know anything else, I know they're in a better place together.

Momma's Celebration

Death is as beautiful as life; we simply don't realize it until we're actually home.

May Allah/God be with each and every one of you,
Carla Davis Bonds

My father, Enmanuel Davis Jr/Emmanuel Mohammad

My husband Bo (Vogel) and I

One of my best friends, Mary

My husband Bo

Traci and her doll

My brothers, from the top; Byron, Craig, Bruce, Mark and Rodney

My daughter, Shelby's graduation from Lindenwood University

Momma, me and Traci

My brother Craig

Janelle, Mary, Karl and Ava

Shelby and I at Traci's for Halloween

Shelby and Johronda at the pool

My cousin Flipsy, brother
Mark and cousin Benny
(Easter pic at Aunt Dorothy and
Uncle Sung's house).

First row, cousin Benetta,
Renee, unknown

Second row, me and
another cousin.

My youngest brother, Rodney

A.G. Edwards sponsored Khory League
team Eric Thomas (Coach)

Traci and Momma at
Traci's 8th graduation

Rodney and Shelby

My mother's youngest brother Gregory and youngest sister, Roslyn

My Brother Craig

My mother's sister Marva

Karl performing in one of many productions

My husband Bo's siblings, Mossie Jr., Bo, Karry, Larry and Ellis, Marvin, Diane and Faye

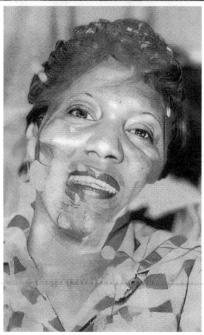

My grandmother Mary

Me, Yolonda, Pam and Ava

My brother Mark

My brother Byron

Dell, Pat
and me

Our Great Aunt Dorothy, Bo and Shelby
Upper row, my brother Craig, Byron, Bruce,
Traci's daughter Johronda.

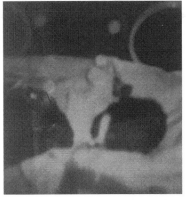

Shelby inside NICU

Aunt Dorothy and Uncle Sung

Yolonda

Bo and Shelby

Traci and her
daughter Johronda

My mother's sister Janice

My grandfather on my mother's side. Boss and Savanah Maddox

My mother's brother Harold

Shelby's 25th birthday (Spa Day)

Our protectors as teenagers, our brother's from other mothers.
Harry, Calvin, Michael and James

Alice, Dell, Juliette and me dressed up and cuttin' up.

Yours truly, me

Aunt Que

Shelby, my father and Johronda

Fred, one of Bo's closets
and longtime friends

Yolonda, Pam and Janelle

Karl and Mary

Laclede Town   One of the many meeting places for the adults

Shelby's Fontbonne University "Drive by/Covid" celebration

Angie made it to the Olympics

Halloween fun times

We began having BET Parties in 2003

Me after waking up on a Saturday to realize that Shelby had been born the previous Thursday. Before I was pregnant, I weighed approx. 130 pounds. I ended up getting toxemia and gained over 70 pounds. It was definitely worth the pain to end up with such a beautiful person. She's exactly what I have been waiting for. My prayers were answered.

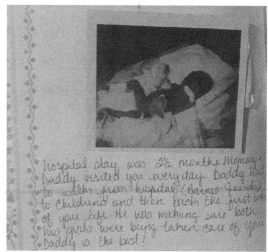

Shelby inside the NICU Dept.

Momma's celebration of Life

Mark, Gene, Bookie and Traci

Byron's Kindergarten class room

Shelby's 25th Spa Birthday Party.

Kaitlyn, Shelby, Nae and Johronda.
Spa bags of robes, slippers and other goodies.

Shelby, Lindenwood Graduation,
Masters in Early Autism Intervention and
Sensory Impairment

Johronda's UMSL graduation with Cam.

Traci, me and Shelby at Johronda's
UMSL graduation

Byron and his shenanigans. Dressed
for work as a leprechaun.

Sleepy, Craig and Daddy

The one and only queen of us all, momma.

Bruce has a son, Kyle, who's a body builder. Here we are attending one of his events. His sister Kellie, Traci, me, Bruce and his wife Diane. Shelby and momma.

I had retired as a Reading Fellow however, kept in touch with the school. For Black History Month, they asked me to record a message from a famous figure. I've always loved Harriet Tubman and sent them a message from her.

Shelby won Prom Queen at her high school. Mark asked that Traci and I bring her to him so he could see and take a picture together.

Byron's shenanigans. Oompa-Loompa costume for work.

Dale. One of the earliest
friends of our family. Over
50 years of friendship.

My father and Stokely Carmichael
(**Kwame Ture),** a prominent
organizer in the civil rights
movement in the United States and
the global pan-African movement.

Articles and pictures from Laclede Town's Newspaper, The Intelligencer

WELL WISHES

Friends and neighbors of the Tenion family were deeply concerned about Bantu's accident.

Bantu's face was burned from an exploding firecracker. As of this writing though, I know everyone will be glad to hear that Bantu's eyesight will be A.O.K.

Take care, Bantu— We look forward to seeing you around and about as usual.

BRIGHT HORIZONS AHEAD

Wardell Thacker, LaClede Town Youth Sports President, states, "the purpose of the Youth Sports is to see that every able bodied child can participate in the sport of his or her choice." Even though this means more money and volunteers, he believes that it is very much worth a person's time and money to help a child in athletics.

With the new fields being made in LaClede West, this should open up a whole new era for Youth Sports. The fields will give the LaClede teams a home field upon which they may play their home regular season games, where as now they must play on neutral fields. Also, people who have to drive 40 blocks now, will only have to walk across the street to see their teams in action.

Coach Bernard Jackson of The Chic Division LaClede Town LUV, ages 10-12 years, are holding the record of 5-4, having lost one to CSMAC and 3 times to our neighboring Bluemeyer Girls team. According to Coach Bernard Jackson, this team has not enjoyed the success that was anticipated, but the girls are looking forward to next year.

The Roster includes: Claudia Stevenson (1.b.) *Felicia Hinton* (2.b.), Kim Hunt (Pitcher), *Monica Shearburn (s.c.),* Angela Brown (3.b.), Alaine Bradly (Catcher), *Kathy Collins* (l.f.), Jackie Williams (s.s.), Rhonda Carr (s.c.), Rhonda Smith (Pitcher), Christina Jackson (Bat Girl).

Manager W Thacker and W. Shearburn

Black Artist Group in Paris

An exciting, landmark concert given by B.A.G. at the Palace Theatre in Paris, France during the Spring of 1973. Personell: Joe Bowie, Baikida Carroll, Oliver Lake, Floyd LeFlore, Charles 'Bobo' Shaw.

WHY THE DRUM?
by Sara Meehan

On a sunny day in Laclede Town several years ago, I heard the pulsating rhythm of a Congo Drum beckoning to me and touching the depths of my soul. I felt my feet barely touch the ground as I flowed toward the sound filling the air.

I opened a door, looked up and saw all of Africa pass before my eyes. With hands faster than the speed of light and energy more dynamic than bolts of lightning and sounds matching my heartbeat to that of the universal heartbeat; I saw HIM playing the Congo drum as if it were the only, first, and last form of expression known to man . . . HE was MOR THIAM, Drummer "Extrodinaire," from Senegal.

To understand what percussion classes mean to me is to first understand the "Sun-god" who is passing his art form on to those who seek him out.

Mor Thiam is both a prophet in his own time and a man of total talent who does not (but could) isolate himself from the world and join only those few who could ever approach his level of excellence: Yet, he chooses to share his art and more: He shares his soul with the students, he is at the same time both performer and teacher.

CONGRATULATIONS TO . . .

Miss Linda Fisher of Grand Towers will be a participant in a program given by the St. Peter's youth choir on Sunday, July 28th at 8:30 p.m. on KMOX-TV, Channel 4. Tune in everyone!

Miss Sharron Harrell of Grand Forest has been accepted for the fall semester at Tarkio College in the Northwest corner of the state. Job well done, Sharron!

THE POOL TABLE COMETH

On March 26, 1974, Manny Davis and Coz went a-buying. What was purchased was the long-awaited standard size pool table, and 2 regulation ping-pong tables.

Coz, Activity Board Chairman and Manny, Director of Community Management took time and consideration in their final choice of tables for our community residents. Manny stated, "we wanted tables that would withstand a lot of stress and strain along with wear and tear. I look for durability because this equipment will see lots of use."

Coz, speaking as Board Chairman stated, "When it comes to spending money that has been provided by others, I like to see the best buy for the initial investment. The choices made by Manny and me, as charged by the Board, suggest good thinking and compromise. The original request was for smaller tables. I felt that we should have regulation size or as near as possible to include the adult segment of the community."

Manny and Coz had plenty of help putting up the tables the same day that they were purchased. The youth of the community were directly involved in this kind of chore. They weren't asked, they just pitched in and helped. Manny has stated many times, "our kids are good kids. I know, I see them all the time."

Coz said, "I like to think that people are basically well meaning and basically good. With youth I prefer to take that attitude. There MUST be room for growth and learning."

When the table was placed into the Art Room at the Peacock Alley Institute, it was noted that in order to bring all the equipment in, most of the maintenance personnel were needed. It was close to quitting time, yet all the guys stayed over to help the center staff erect the tables and sample the pool table felt with a game or two.

(editor's note: It's a warm feeling to know that even though the men were tired and ready to go, they were willing to give "a little something extra" of themselves. As you look at the pictures that were taken of the event, you'll see that there was lots of COMMUNITY involvement by all concerned. A tip of the hat to MANNY DAVIS and to COZ, for "getting it together." A thank you from the residents, both young and old to our field operations men for lending a hand. And to the kids who were a part of the construction . . . keep on, keepin' on.)

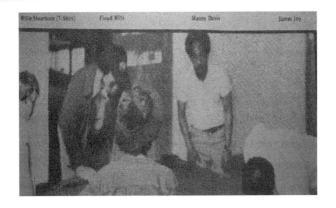

WHY THE DRUM?
by Sara Meehan

On a sunny day in Laclede Town several years ago, I heard the pulsating rhythm of a Congo Drum beckoning to me and touching the depths of my soul. I felt my feet barely touch the ground as I flowed toward the sound filling the air.

I opened a door, looked up and saw all of Africa pass before my eyes, with hands faster than the speed of light, and energy more dynamic than bolts of lightning and sounds matching my heartbeat to that of the universal heartbeat: I saw HIM playing the Congo drum as if it were the only, first, and last form of expression known to man . . . HE was MOR THIAM, Drummer "Extrodinaire," from Senegal.

To understand what percussion classes mean to me is to first understand the "Sun-god" who is passing his art form on to those who seek him out.

Mor Thiam is both a prophet in his own time and a man of total talent who does not (but could) isolate himself from the world and join only those few who could ever approach his level of excellence: Yet, he chooses to share his art and more: He shares his soul with the students, he is at the same time both performer and teacher.

CONGRATULATIONS TO . . .

Miss Linda Fisher of Grand Towers will be a participant in a program given by the St. Peter's youth choir on Sunday, July 28th at 8:30 p.m. on KMOX-TV, Channel 4. Tune in everyone!

Miss Sharron Harrell of Grand Forest has been accepted for the fall semester at Tarkio College in the Northwest corner of the state. Job well done, Sharron!

THE POOL TABLE COMETH

On March 28, 1974, Manny Davis and Coz went a-buying. What was purchased was the long awaited standard size pool table, and 2 regulation ping-pong tables.

Coz, Activity Board Chairman and Manny, Director of Community Management took time and consideration in their final choices of tables for our community residents. Manny stated, "we wanted tables that would withstand a lot of stress and strain along with wear and tear. I look for durability because this equipment will see lots of use."

Coz, speaking as Board Chairman stated, "When it comes to spending money that has been provided by others, I like to see the best buy for the initial investment. The choices made by Manny and me, as charged by the Board, suggest good thinking and compromise. The original request was for smaller tables. I felt that we should have regulation size or as near as possible to include the adult segment of the community."

Manny and Coz had plenty of help putting up the tables the same day that they were purchased. The youth of the community were directly involved in this kind of chore. They weren't asked, they just pitched in and helped. Manny has stated many times, "our kids are good kids. I know, I see them all the time."

Coz said, "I like to think that people are basically well meaning and basically good. With youth I prefer to take that attitude. There MUST be room for growth and learning."

When the table was placed into the Art Room at the Peacock Alley Institute, it was noted that in order to bring all the equipment in, most of the maintenance personnel were needed. It was close to quitting time, yet all the guys stayed over to help the center staff erect the tables and sample the pool table felt with a game or two.

[editor's note: It's a warm feeling to know that even though the men were tired and ready to go, they were willing to give "a little something extra" of themselves. As you look at the pictures that were taken of the event, you'll see that there was lots of COMMUNITY involvement by all concerned. A tip of the hat to MANNY DAVIS and to COZ, for "getting it together." A thank you from the residents, both young and old to our field operations men for lending a hand. And to the kids who were a part of the construction . . . Keep on, keepin' on.]

Willie Shearburn (T-Shirt)   Floyd Wills   Manny Davis   James Joy

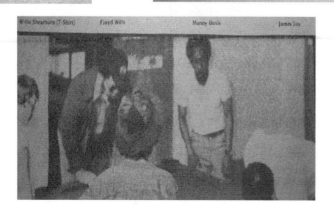

We are here on this earth for a short time. During our stay, all of us must acknowledge that without the right upbringing, we will perish and our lives here on this planet would have been in vain. Live your lives righteously and to the fullest. Yes, mistakes will be made, tears will fall, life will bring you difficulties. Difficulties are failures, and failures are what makes you grow to become the best you can be. At the end of it all, the almighty will question you as to what did you do to better someone else's journey. I hope with all my heart, that your answer will be enough to enter the gates of eternity. Peace

be with you.

My parents, Mr. and Mrs. Davis (Emmanuel Davis Jr. and Edythe Wynn)
Death is as beautiful as life; we simply don't realize it until we're actually home.

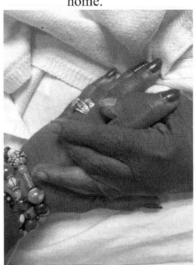

Ethel Blanks was born in March 1890 in Missouri. She had one daughter with Ah Sing in 1920.

Spouse	Ah Sing
Children	Que Y
Birth	Mar 1890 Missouri, USA

Ethel's family

Ah Sing had one son Louis and one daughter Que with Ethel Blanks in 1920.

Children: Que Y Sing: born on April 2, 1920, in St Louis, Missouri. Passed away on June 29, 1998, in St Louis, Missouri, at the age of 78.

Household Members (Name)	Age	Relationship
Ethel Anderson	36	Head
Waneta Anderson	14	Daughter
Floyd Anderson	12	Son
Queying Sing	10	Son
Song Sing	8	Son

Name	Godi Jok
Age	58
Birth Year	abt 1862
Birthplace	China
Home in 1920	St Louis Ward 20, St Louis (Independent City), Missouri
Street	Vandeventer Ave
House Number	712
Residence Date	1920
Race	Chinese
Gender	Male
Immigration Year	1881[1891]
Relation to Head of House	Head
Marital Status	Single
Father's Birthplace	China
Mother's Birthplace	China
Native Tongue	Chinese
Able to Speak English	Yes
Occupation	Manager
Industry	Laundry

Household Members (Name)	Age	Relationship
Godi Jok	58	Head
Ethel Anderson	28	Servant
Elmer Anderson	12	Lodger
Irma Anderson	8	Lodger

U.S., World War II Draft Cards Young Men, 1940-1947 for Louis Sing Missouri

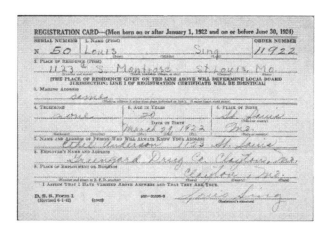

Name	Louis Sing
Gender	Male
Birth Date	29 Mar 1922
Death Date	31 Jan 2014
Cemetery	Jefferson Barracks National-Cemetery Plot: Sect 1-IIB site 103B-

Memorial ID: 146546289

Burial   Lemay, St. Louis County, Missouri,

Name: Fooyon Sing

Age	23
Birth Year	abt 1897
Birthplace	Arkansas
Home in 1920	St Louis MO
Street	Lawton Ave
Residence Date	1920
Race	Black
Gender	Male
Relation to Head of House	Roomer
Industry	Furs
Employment Field	Wage or Salary
Able to read	Yes
Able to Write	Yes
Neighbors	View others on page

SERIAL NUMBER	1. NAME (Print)			ORDER NUMBER
294	FLOYD	—	ANDERSON	V 2055
	(First)	(Middle)	(Last)	

2. ADDRESS (Print) 313 SOUTH GRAND AVE St Louis MO
(Number and street or R. F. D. number) (Town) (County) (State)

3. TELEPHONE	4. AGE IN YEARS	5. PLACE OF BIRTH	6. COUNTRY OF CITIZENSHIP
None	22	St Louis	USA
	DATE OF BIRTH		
—	AUG 31 1918	MO	
(Exchange) (Number)	(Mo.) (Day) (Yr.)	(State or country)	

7. NAME OF PERSON WHO WILL ALWAYS KNOW YOUR ADDRESS
Mrs ETHEL — ANDERSON
(First) (Middle) (Last)

8. RELATIONSHIP OF THAT PERSON MOTHER

9. ADDRESS OF THAT PERSON 1123 SOUTH MONTROSE St Louis MO
(Number and street or R. F. D. number) (Town) (County) (State)

10. EMPLOYER'S NAME CARR Laundry Co

11. PLACE OF EMPLOYMENT OR BUSINESS 3319 Market St
(Number and street or R. F. D. number) (Town) (County) (State)

I AFFIRM THAT I HAVE VERIFIED ABOVE ANSWERS AND THAT THEY ARE TRUE.

REGISTRATION CARD
D. S. S. Form 1   (over)   16—17103

Floyd Anderson
(Registrant's signature)

73

Household Members	Age	Relationships
Ethel Anderson	57	Head
Juanita Davis	34	Daughter
Emmanuel Davis	15	Grandson
Michael Davis	3	Grandson
Floyd Anderson	31	Son
Tueying Jones	30	Daughter
Jerald Jones	11	Grandson
Veronica Jones	9	Granddaughter
Louis Sing	28	Son
Dorothy Sing	21	Daughter in Law
Linda J Sing	1	Granddaughter

Household Members (Name)	Age	Relationship
Godi Jok	58	Head
Ethel Anderson	28	Servant
Elmer Anderson	12	Lodger
Irma Anderson	8	Lodger

My mother)

Edith Louise Wynn   B: April 6, 1940   D: November 19, 2021

Spouse: Manuel Davis B: March 16, 1934   D: July 25, 2016

Children

Mark Davis	B: Aril 9, 1958
Carla Davis	B: August 19, 1959
Craig Davis	B: July 30, 1960
Bruce Davis	B: June 30, 1961
Byron Davis	B: January 6, 1962
Traci Davis	B: November 23, 1964
Rodney Davis	B: July 25, 1965

Name: Obadiah William Wynn (My mother's father)

Death Age: 63

Birth Date: 18 Sep 1916

Service Date: Start 7 Aug 1945

Service Date End   17 Dec 1945

Death Date: 24 Dec 1979

Interment Date: 31 Dec 1979

Interment: Missouri, USA

Cemetery Address 2900 Sheridan Road St. Louis, MO 63125

Cemetery Jefferson Barracks National Cemetery

Plot   Section Q Site 1224 Plot: Q01224 Memorial ID: 81349399

Name	Obediah Wynn
Birth Year	abt 1916
Gender	Male
Race	Negro (Black)
Age in 1930	13
Birthplace	Mississippi
Marital Status	Single
Relation to Head of House	Son
Home in 1930	St Louis, St. Louis (Independent City), Missouri, USA
Map of Home	St Louis, St. Louis (Independent City), Missouri
Street Address	Chouteau Avenue
Ward of City	Sixth Pt
Block	1261
House Number	2802
Dwelling Number	121
Family Number	2
Attended School	Yes
Able to Read and Write	Yes
Father's Birthplace	Mississippi
Mother's Birthplace	Mississippi
Able to Speak English	Yes

Household Members (Name)	Age	Relationship
John Wynn	51	Head
Rena Wynn	49	Wife
John Wynn	19	Son
Theopplus Wynn	17	Son
Dorothy Wynn	16	Daughter
Nannie Davis	21	Daughter
Irene Davis	0	Granddaughter
Obediah Wynn	13	Son

SERIAL NUMBER 1438

1. NAME (Print) WILLIAM Obadiah WYNN
(First) (Middle) (Last)

ORDER NUMBER 903

2. ADDRESS (Print) 1103½ Ohio ST Louis Mo
(Number and street or R. F. D. number) (Town) (County) (State)

3. TELEPHONE ✓ ✓
(Exchange) (Number)

4. AGE IN YEARS 24
DATE OF BIRTH Sept 18 1916
(Mo.) (Day) (Yr.)

5. PLACE OF BIRTH STARKSVILLE
(Town or county)
MISS
(State or country)

6. COUNTRY OF CITIZENSHIP

7. NAME OF PERSON WHO WILL ALWAYS KNOW YOUR ADDRESS
MRS RENA — WYNN
(Mr., Mrs., Miss) (First) (Middle) (Last)

8. RELATIONSHIP OF THAT PERSON MOTHER

9. ADDRESS OF THAT PERSON 4226 West LabadiE ST Louis Mo
(Number and street or R. F. D. number) (Town) (County) (State)

10. EMPLOYER'S NAME PARAMOUNT SHOE MANUFACTURING Co

11. PLACE OF EMPLOYMENT OR BUSINESS 4164—72 Chippiwa ST Louis Mo
(Number and street or R. F. D. number) (Town) (County) (State)

I AFFIRM THAT I HAVE VERIFIED ABOVE ANSWERS AND THAT THEY ARE TRUE.

REGISTRATION CARD
D. S. S. Form 1 (over) 16—17108

William Obadiah Wynn
(Registrant's signature)

Name	Charles Wynn (Obadiah's grandfather)
Age	50
Birth Date	Abt May 1850
Birthplace	Mississippi, USA
Home in 1900	Beat 5, Oktibbeha, Mississippi
Sheet Number	15
Number of Dwelling in Order of Visitation	291
Family Number	303
Race	Black
Gender	Male
Relation to Head of House	Head
Marital Status	Married
Spouse's Name	Ella Wynn (Obadiah's grandmother)
Marriage Year	1870
Years Married	30
Father's Birthplace	Tennessee, USA

Household Members (Name)	Age	Relationship
Charles Wynn B: 1848- 1922 (Obadiah's grandfather)	50	Head
Ella Wynn B: 1858-1927 Obadiah's grandmother)	41	Wife
John Wynn (1879 Obadiah's father	21	Son
Albert Wynn 7-27-1880 D: 11-8-19662 82yrs old (Uncle)	19	Son
Rose Bud Wynn B: 12-882 D: 1966 (Aunt)	17	Daughter
Asa Wynn 4-1883 (Uncle)	17	Son
Bevy Wynn 6-1887 (Uncle)	12	Son
Wolsey Wynn (Uncle)	9	Son
Lelia Wynn 1894-1969 (Aunt)	7	Daughter
Seanie Wynn 1896 (Aunt)	4	Daughter

Name	Emanuel Davis (Daddy's father)
Respondent	Yes
Age	25
Estimated Birth Year	abt 1915
Gender	Male
Race	Negro (Black)
Birthplace	Missouri
Marital Status	Married
Relation to Head of House	Head
Home in 1940	St Louis, St Louis City, Missouri
Map of Home in 1940	St Louis, St Louis City, Missouri
Street	Easton Avenue
House Number	4121
Farm	No
Inferred Residence in 1935	St Louis, St Louis City, Missouri
Residence in 1935	St Louis
Resident on farm in 1935	No
Sheet Number	1B
Number of Household in Order of Visitation	15
Occupation	Elevator Operator
House Owned or Rented	Rented
Highest grade completed	High School, 3rd year

Household Members (Name)	Age	Relationship
Emanuel Davis	25	Head
Juanita Davis	24	Wife
Jacquelyn Davis	6	Daughter
Emanuel Davis	5	Son
Julia Anderson	66	Aunt

Household Members (Name)	Age	Relationship
Boss Maddox (birth year same)?	35	Head
Cora (Corrine Maddox)	33	Wife
Mary Maddox	11	Daughter

Name	Boss Maddox
Gender	Male
Age	22
Birth Year	abt 1895
Residence	Tillar Drew, Ark
Spouse's name	Cora Brooks
Spouse's Age	22
Spouse's Residence	Tillar Drew, Ark
Marriage Date	11/29/1917
Marriage License Date	11/29/1917
Event Type	Marriage

MARRIAGE LICENSE

(Coupon to be Detached by County Clerk and Forwarded to State Registrar Vital Statistics, State Capitol)

State of Arkansas

Desha

Boss Maddox .... of Tillar

Drew .... State of Arkansas .... and

22 .... Nationality Negro

Cora Brooks .... of Tillar

Drew .... State of Arkansas

22 .... Nationality Negro

12th day of November 19 17.

_____ County Clerk

_____ Deputy County Clerk

Name	Boss Maddox	Name	Mary Louise Maddox/Wynn
Gender	Male	Gender	Female
Spouse	Corrine M Brooks	Race	Black
Child	Mary Louise Wynn	Birth Date	2 Sep 1918
		Birth Place	Tillar, Arkansas
		Death Date	4 Aug 1991
		Father	Boss Maddox
		Mother	Corrine M Brooks

84

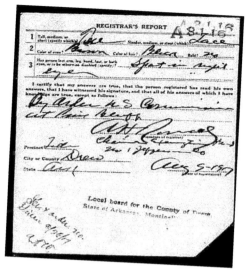

U.S., World War I Draft Registration Cards, 1917-1918 for Boss Maddox

Name: Boss Maddox
Birth Year abt 1895 D: June 1984 (90 years old)

Gender: Male

Race: Negro (Black)

Age in 1930: 35

Birthplace: Louisiana

Marital Status: Married

Relation to Head of House: Head

Home in 1930 St Louis, (Independent City), Missouri, USA

Street Address   Cardinal Ave
Ward of City   16th pt

```
┌─────────────────────────────────────────────────────┐
│                                                     │
│   Boss Maddox's parents                             │
│                                                     │
│      Father's Birthplace              Louisiana     │
│                                                     │
│      Mother's Birthplace              Louisiana     │
│                                                     │
│      Able to Speak English            Yes           │
│                                                     │
│                                                     │
│      Occupation                       Laborer       │
│                                                     │
│                                                     │
└─────────────────────────────────────────────────────┘
```

Selected person: Seanie Wynn

Parents: My great-great grandparents Charley and Ella Wynn

Birth: Aug 1895 • Mississippi; Residence: 1900 • Beat 5, Oktibbeha, Mississippi, USA, Marital Status: Single; Relation to Head: Daughter; Residence: 1910 • Starkville Ward 3, Oktibbeha, Mississippi, USA, Marital Status: Single; Relation to Head of House: Daughter

Life Events: Seanie Wynn was born in August 1985 in Missississippi to Ella Wynn, age 37, and Charley Wynn, age 46. Seanie Wynn lived in Okitibbeha, Mississippi in 1900. Marital Status: Single; Relation to Head: Daughter. In 1910, Seanie was 15 years old and lived in Starksville, Mississippi. In 1913, Seanie's half-sister, Mattie died. Mattie was 18 years old. In 1922, Seanie's father died at the age of 73. Ella passed away in 1927 at the age of 69. In 1962, Seanie's half-brother, Albert died in November. Seanie was 67 years old. Her half-brother, Asa died in 1967. In 1966, Seanie's half-sister Rosebud died on November 2, 1966 in Armory, Mississippi. Seanie was 71 years old. Her half-sister Lelia died in 1969 when Seanie was 74 years old. In 1973, Seanie's half-sister Sean L. died in January in Starksville, Mississippi. Seanie was 77 years old. In 1974, Seanie's half-brother Walter Walsey died on April 13th in Missouri. Seaanie was 78 years old. Her half-brother John, my great grandfather, died in January 1975 in St. Louis, Missouri. Seanie was 80 years old. Ella died in 1927. Charley died in 1922

Name	Cora Brooks (My mother's grand
Age in 1910	12
Birth Date	1898[1898]
Birthplace	Arkansas
Home in 1910	Clayton, Desha, Arkansas, USA
Sheet Number	13a
Race	Black
Gender	Female
Relation to Head of House	Daughter
Marital Status	Single
Father's Name	Edward Brooks
Father's Birthplace	Virginia
Mother's Name	Mary A Brooks
Mother's Birthplace	Mississippi
Native Tongue	English
Occupation	Farm Laborer
Industry	Home Farm
Employer, Employee or Other	Wage Earner

Household Members
(Name)   Age Relationship
_____

Edward Brooks   52   Head

Mary A Brooks   33   Wife

Sallie Brooks   17   Daughter

John Brooks   16   Son

Curtie Brooks   15   Son

Cora Brooks   12   Daughter

Lula Brooks   10   Daughter

Amanda Brooks   9   Daughter

Mary A. Dorch (Brooks) – Cora's mother/my great-great grandmother

Born: April 17, 1869/Tillar, Arkansas

Mary's children;

Son, George Dorch	Born: 1874

Daughter, Sallie Dorch   Born: 1876

Son, Isaac Dorch	Born: 1879	Died: 1932

Son, Dave Dorch	Born: 1883	Died: 1943

Marriage: 26 Dec 1889 • Desha, Arkansas, United States Edward E Brooks

Son, John Brooks	Born: 1892	Died: 1936

Daughter, Elizabeth Sallie Born: 1893	Died: 1951

Son, Curtis "Kirk"	Born: 1893	Died: 1967

Daughter, Cora	Born: 1897	Died: 1940

Daughter, Lula   Born: 1898   Died: 1968

Daughter, Amanda   Born: 1901   Died: 1985

Daughter, Leola	Born: 1903	Died: 1996

When Our mother died
This Dear lady slepted
up to the Plate for us
and she hit a home run
for us. But to be sure
we will see ogin in the
Resurrection (MARY ALICE
BROOKS

Yes, the ultimate solution rests with our Creator. He alone can fully remove suffering, reverse the effects of sin, and undo death. Jesus Christ told his disciples about an outstanding development that is yet ahead of us. He said: "The hour is coming in which all those in the memorial tombs will hear his voice and come out."—John 5:28, 29.

| Mary A Brooks | Born: April 17, 1869, Tillar, Arkansas |
| | Died: 27 Sep 1954 • Tillar, Desha, Arkansas, USA |

Mary A Brooks

BIRTH: April 17, 1869

DEATH: September 27, 1954

BURIAL

Seven Star Cemetery

Reed, Desha County, Arkansas, USA

MEMORIAL ID: 18895178

My Great-great grandmother Mary A. Dorch (Brooks) son and my great-great Uncle Curtis' Birth Certificate

Name	Edward Brooks
Gender	Male
Race	Black
Death Age	80
Birth Date	25 Dec 1848
Death Date	11 Aug 1929
Death Place	Petersburg, Dinwiddie, Virginia, USA
Registration Date	13 Aug 1929
Spouse	Mary Brooks
Certificate Number	1929019767

Great-great grandfather Edward Brooks, death certificate. Note: Indicate birth date 12-25-1848

THE END

Made in the USA
Monee, IL
02 August 2024

5c63ee2c-41d2-4cd1-b840-0b1290c67593R01